Rosa Parks

By Mary Nhin

Illustrated By
Yuliia Zolotova

Hi, I'm Rosa Parks.

I grew up in a time of segregation, where black children like me couldn't get a bus to school that was designated for white children. Unfortunately, school bus transportation was unavailable in any form for black school children in the South.

Arsonists tried to burn my school down twice just because they didn't want black children to get an education.

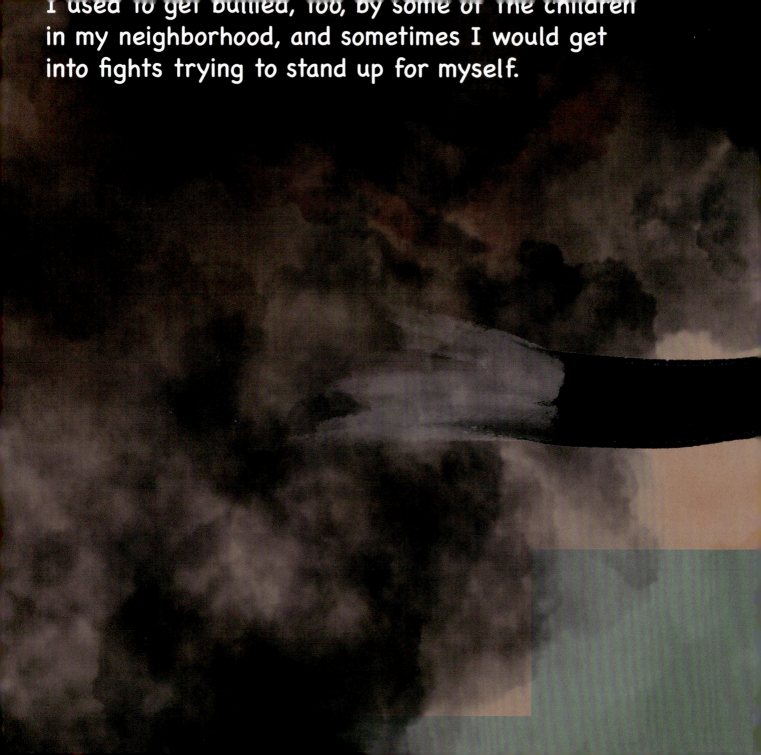

I used to get bullied, too, by some of the children in my neighborhood, and sometimes I would get into fights trying to stand up for myself.

In time, I got married to a wonderful man. My husband was a civil rights supporter, and I joined his campaign. We believed in equal justice and we were committed to achieving it, too.

The lack of justice for people of color and the daily mistreatment that I observed and endured was too much to bear.

One day, I boarded a bus and paid the fare. I chose a seat, but the driver told me to follow city rules and enter the bus again from the back door. When I exited the vehicle, the bus driver drove off without me. I was really sad about it.

Another day, I resisted being kicked out of a bus seat to make room for a man just because he was white. I refused to move and the bus driver had me arrested, though I had committed no crime.

My arrest sent a message to people loud and clear and a boycott of the buses began. People demanded fairness.

Today's mighty oak tree is yesterday's nut that held its ground.

I became a very famous face in the civil rights movement, which of course also attracted a lot of negative attention from people.

But the more they tried to silence me, the more outraged we became. We began a campaign called the Montgomery Bus Boycott which proved to be effective.

My work ended segregation on public transport, and I devoted my whole life to campaigning for equality. Though I'd been afraid, I did what I knew was right and it changed the world.

I believe we are here on the planet Earth to live, grow up and do what we can to make this world a better place for all people to enjoy freedom.

Timeline

1955 – Rosa famously refused to give up
           her bus seat to a white passenger

1987 – Founded the Rosa and Raymond Parks
           Institute for Self Development

1996 – Rosa was awarded the Presidential
           Medal of Freedom

1999 – Rosa was awarded the Congressional Gold Medal

minimovers.tv